Student Workbook to Accompany

Intercultural Communication
A Contextual Approach

2nd Edition

Student Workbook to Accompany

Intercultural Communication
A Contextual Approach
2nd Edition

James W. Neuliep
St. Norbert College

Houghton Mifflin Company   Boston   New York

Sponsoring Editor: Adam Forrand
Associate Editor: Kristen Desmond LeFevre
Editorial Associate: Brigitte Maser
Associate Project Editor: Kristin Penta
Senior Manufacturing Coordinator: Jane Spelman
Marketing Manager: Barbara Lebuhn

Printed in the U.S.A.

ISBN: 0-618-21856-4

123456789—EW—06 05 04 03 02

Table of Contents

Chapter One:
The Necessity of Intercultural Communication

Chapter Overview:

The major thrust of Chapter One is that the population of the United States is becoming racially and ethnically diverse, thus creating a need for intercultural communication. Moreover, there are several benefits to becoming competent intercultural communicators, including:

-healthier communities
-increased commerce
-reduced conflict, and
-personal growth.

The chapter begins by discussing the need for and benefits of intercultural communication. The chapter then profiles the latest U.S. Census data regarding population growth since 1990. The data indicates that the U.S. population is becoming increasingly diverse. The chapter then goes into an extended discussion of human communication, human communication apprehension, and culture. Next, the contextual model of intercultural communication is presented. The chapter ends with a discussion of intercultural communication apprehension and three fundamental assumptions about intercultural communication.

Chapter Outline (based on chapter headings)

I. The Need for Intercultural Communication
   A. The Benefits of Intercultural Communication
   B. Diversity in the United States
   C. Human Communication

II. The Nature of Human Communication
   A. Dimension 1: Process
   B. Dimension 2: Dynamic
   C. Dimension 3: Interactive/Transactive
   D. Dimension 4: Symbolic
   E. Dimension 5: Intentional
   F. Dimension 6: Contextual
   G. Dimension 7: Ubiquitous
   H. Dimension 8: Cultural

III. Human Communication Apprehension

IV. The Nature of Culture
A. Culture as an accumulated pattern of values, beliefs, and behaviors
B. Culture as an identifiable group of people with a common history
C. Culture as a verbal and nonverbal symbol system
D. Microcultural Groups

V. A Contextual Model of Intercultural Communication

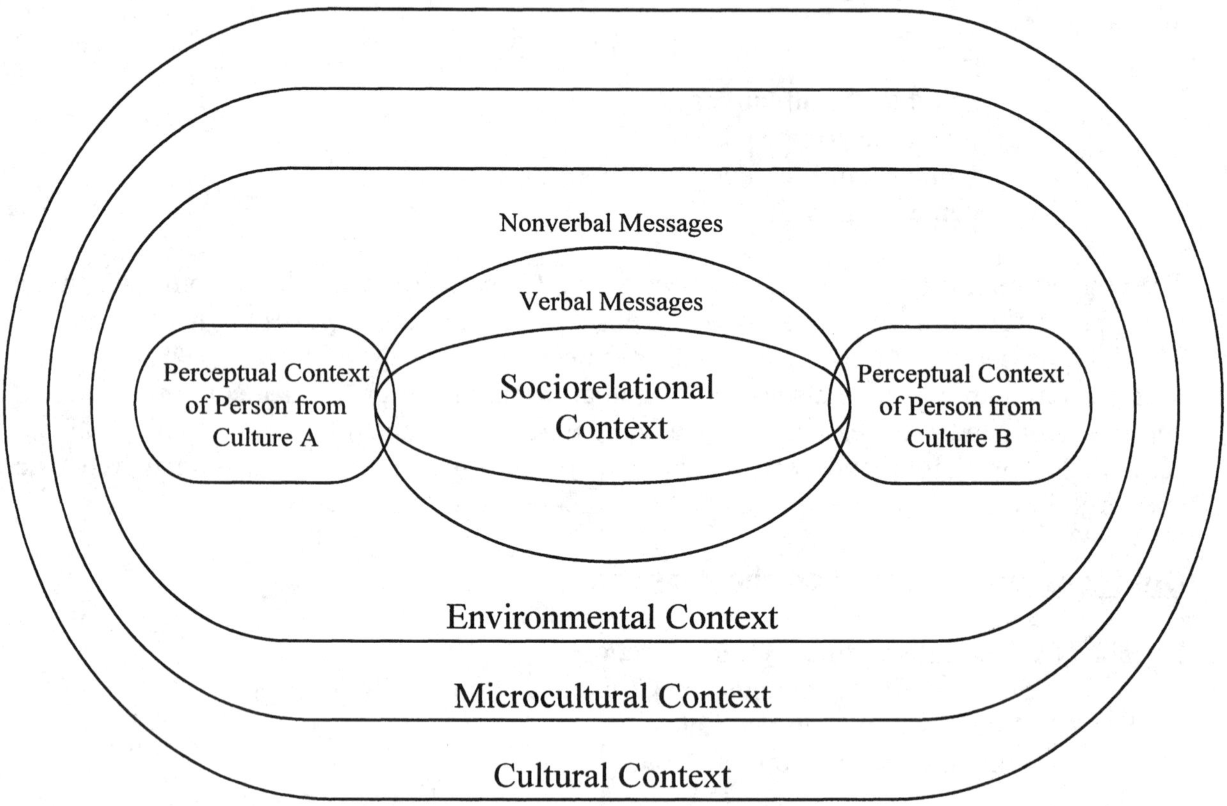

A. Intercultural Communication and Uncertainty
B. Intercultural Communication Apprehension

VI. Fundamental Assumptions About Intercultural Communication
A. Assumption 1: During Intercultural communication, the message sent is not the message received
B. Assumption 2: Intercultural communication is primarily a nonverbal act between people
C. Assumption 3. Intercultural communication necessarily involves a clash of communicator styles

VII. Chapter Summary

Review of Key Concepts

Culture: An accumulated pattern of values, beliefs, and behaviors shared by an identifiable group of people with a common history and verbal and nonverbal symbol system.

Human Communication: The cultural, ubiquitous, contextual, intentional, symbolic, interactive, transactive, and dynamic process of people coming together to exchange verbal and nonverbal messages.

Human Communication Apprehension: The fear or anxiety associated with either real or anticipated communication with others.

Intercultural Communication Apprehension: The fear or anxiety associated with either real or anticipated communication with people from different cultures or ethnic groups.

Exercises:

1. Knowing Yourself

Chapter One includes three Self-Assessment instruments. If you have not already done so, complete each of them. Write your scores below.

Personal Report of Communication Apprehension (PRCA) Score = __________

Based on the scoring procedures, is your PRCA score considered high, moderate, or low? (circle one).

Personal Report of Intercultural Communication Apprehension (PRICA) Score =

____

Based on the scoring procedures, is your PRICA score considered high, moderate, or low? (circle one).

Generalized Ethnocentrism (GENE) Score = __________

Based on the scoring procedures, is your GENE score considered high, moderate, or low? (circle one).

In the space provided below, write down some of the reasons why you think your score is high, moderate, or low for each of the Self-Assessment instruments.

PRCA

PRICA

GENE

2. **Mini Census**

Chapter One provides data about the growing racial and ethnic diversity of the United States. After reviewing that data, conduct your own mini-census. Find a place on your campus where you can observe students, faculty, and staff and count the number of people in the following racial/ethnic categories.

	Number Observed	Percentage of Total
African-American	____________	____________
Asian	____________	____________
Hispanic	____________	____________
White	____________	____________
Other	____________	____________
Total Observed	____________	

How do your observations and data compare to the national census data reported in Chapter One? Is your campus more or less representative of the country as a whole?

Examination Preparation:

1. Briefly list and discuss the benefits of intercultural communication.

2. In your own words, define and discuss the three fundamental assumptions about intercultural communication.

3. Define and discuss four of the eight dimensions of communication.

4. Below is a blank copy of the contextual model of intercultural communication. Label each of the circles (contexts).

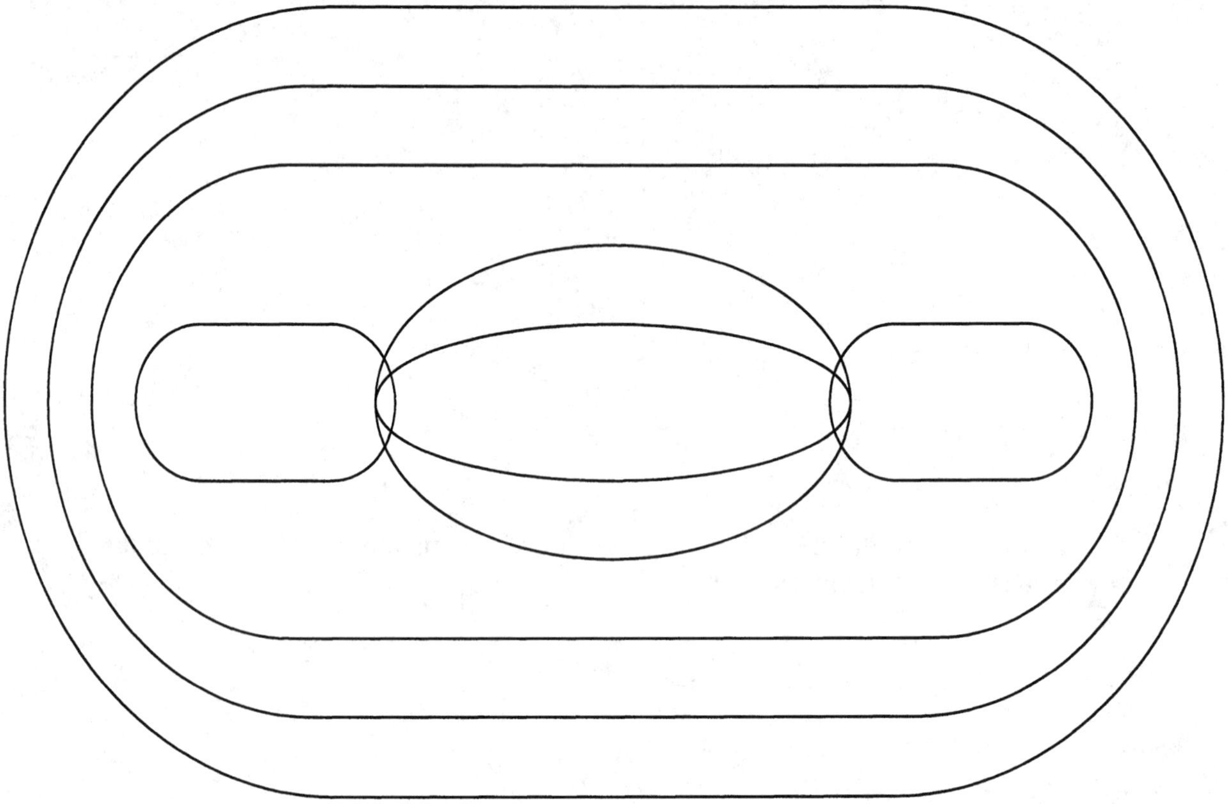

5. In a sentence or two, define the following terms.

Communication apprehension

Intentionality

Uncertainty

Culture

Chapter Two:
The Cultural Context

Chapter Overview:

The central theme of Chapter Two is that the cultural context is perhaps the most defining influence on human communication. The chapter emphasizes that people are not born with a culture. Culture is not like skin color or hair color. Culture is learned. People are taught culture. The chapter also emphasizes that although culture has an immense influence on the way we think, feel, and act, for the most part, we are unconscious of it. In other words, we don't consciously think about what culture we are from as we go about our daily activities. The only time we really actively think about our cultural conditioning is when we travel to a foreign culture, where the people think, feel, and act differently.

Chapter Two attempts to answer the question: What does it mean to say that one culture is different than another? Scholars from across a broad range of disciplines have isolated several *dimensions of cultural variability*, including individualism/collectivism, high/low context, high/low power distance, strong/weak uncertainty avoidance, and value orientations. Chapter Two presents an extended discussion of each of these dimensions of cultural variability. After reading the chapter, you should be able to define and discuss each of one of the dimensions. For each dimension, the chapter also presents an *Intercultural Conversation.* These are short dialogues/scripts of people interacting. Each conversation is designed to demonstrate how the dimension of cultural variability affects human communication. In addition, there are several Self-Assessment instruments for you to complete, so that you can compare yourself with others.

Chapter Outline: (based on chapter headings)

I. Individualism/Collectivism
   A. Consequences of Individualism/Collectivism
   B. Hofstede's Cultural Preferences
   C. Vertical and Horizontal Individualism and Collectivism

II. High-Context/Low Context Communication
   A. Characteristics of High-Context and Low-Context Cultures
   B. Communication Consequences of High-Context and Low-Context Cultural Orientations

III. Value Orientations
   A. Hsu's Postulates of Basic American Values
   B. The Chinese Value Survey
   C. Schwartz's Universal Values
   D. Kluckhohn and Strodtbeck's Value Orientations

IV. Power Distance
   A. Hofstede's Power Distance

V. Uncertainty Avoidance
   A. Hofstede's Uncertainty Avoidance Index

VI. Chapter Summary

Review of Key Concepts

Collectivism: Cultural orientation that the group is the primary unit of culture. Group goals take precedence over individual goals.

High Context: Cultural orientation where meanings are gleaned from the physical, social, and psychological contexts.

Individualism: Cultural orientation that the individual is unique and emphasizing individual goals over group goals.

Low Context: Cultural orientation where meanings are encoded in the verbal code.

Power Distance: The extent to which members of a culture expect and accept that power is unequally distributed.

Uncertainty Avoidance: The degree to which members of a particular culture feel threatened by unpredictable, uncertain, or unknown situations.

Values: Criteria for selecting and justifying behavior. Values have a cognitive, affective, and behavioral component.

Exercises:

1. Review the discussion of individualism in the text and then list three activities in which you engage that are indicative of an individualist orientation. Why/how do you think these are individualistic?

Activity #1 ____

This is individualistic because:

Activity #2 ____

This is individualistic because:

Activity #3 ____

This is individualistic because:

2. Review the discussion of collectivism in the text and then list three activities in which you engage that are indicative of a collectivistic orientation. Why/how do you think these are collectivistic?

Activity #1 ____

This is collectivistic because:

Activity #2 ____

This is collectivistic because:

Activity #3 ____

This is collectivistic because:

3. Below are several statements regarding your general feelings about the nature of things. On a scale of 1 to 5, indicate the degree to which you agree with the statement such that 1 = Strongly Agree, 2 = Agree, 3 = Neutral, 4 = Disagree, and 5 = Strongly Disagree.

1. _____ An individual's self-interest, self-expression, self-improvement, self-gratification, and independence should take precedence over group interests.

2. _____ Children and young adults should be obedient to, and show respect for, their parents.

3. _____ Privacy is the individual's inalienable right. Intrusion into it by others should be permitted only by invitation.

4. _____ On the job and in life loyalty to one's superiors is key.

5. _____ Because the government exists for the benefit of the individual and not vice-versa, all forms of authority, including government, are suspect. Patriotism is good.

6. _____ An individual's success in life depends upon acceptance among his or her peers.

7. _____ If a friend gives me a gift or favor, it is important for me to reciprocate.

8. _____ Moderation, rather than excess, should be practiced in life.

9. _____ An individual should believe in or acknowledge God and should belong to an organized church or another religious institution.

10. _____ A person should know his or her status and respect others who are higher ranking.

11. _____ I try to observe our national holidays and engage in appropriate social rituals.

12. _____ Men and women are equal.

13. _____ All human beings are equal.

14. _____ Progress is good and inevitable. An individual should improve himself/herself (minimize efforts and maximize returns).

15. _____ Keeping myself disinterested and pure is valuable to me.

16. _____ People should have a sense of shame.

17. _____ America is the utmost symbol of progress.

18. _____ People should be content with their position in life.

Score A: Add your responses from items 1, 3, 5, 6, 9, 12, 13, 14, 17.
Score B: Add your responses from items 2, 4, 7, 8, 10, 11, 15, 16, 18.
Compare score A and B. Which is higher?

Items 1, 3, 5, 6, 9, 12, 13, 14, and 17 are taken from Hsu's Postulates of Basic American Values presented in Chapter Two. Items 2, 4, 7, 8, 10, 11, 15, 16, and 18 were taken from the list of 40 Chinese values also presented in Chapter Two. If you were born and raised in the United States, Score A is probably lower than Score B. In this case, a lower score indicates that you tend to agree with those statements.

Examination Preparation

1. Compare and contrast (do both) high vs. low context cultures.

2. What is the difference between a high power distance and a low power distance culture?

3. Identify three countries that possess a generally weak uncertainty avoidant orientation.

4. Identify three countries that possess a generally strong uncertainty avoidant orientation.

5. In a sentence or two, define the following terms:

    Individualism

    Collectivism

    Uncertainty Avoidance

    Power Distance

Chapter Three:
The Microcultural Context

Chapter Overview:

The major idea of Chapter Three is that within most cultures there are groups of people who differ in some way from the general "majority" culture. These groups are sometimes called minorities or subcultures, but in this book they are called microcultures. Microcultures are those identifiable groups of people who share a set of values, beliefs, and behaviors and who possess a common history and verbal and nonverbal symbol system that is similar to the dominant culture but differs in some way, perhaps subtly. Often times microcultures differ in terms of race, ethnicity, language, dress, or religion.

The chapter points out that often microcultures become "muted" within the dominant culture. This means that their ideas are largely overlooked. The language of the microculture is often ignored or discounted by the larger "macro" culture.

There are several microcultures in the United States and, in combination, they make up a sizable percentage of the population. Four microcultural groups are profiled in Chapter Three, including Hispanics/Latinos, African-Americans, Amish, and Hmong. The communication patterns and practices of each group are described.

Chapter Outline (based on chapter headings)

I. Microcultural Group Status

II. Muted Microcultural Groups

III. Microcultural Groups in the United States
- A. Hispanics/Latinos
  1. Cultural Values of Hispanics
  2. Spanglish: A Language of Hispanic Americans
  3. Stereotypes of Hispanics
- B. African-Americans
  1. Black English, Dialect, and Ebonics
  2. The Dozens
  3. The Origins of Black Language
- C. The Amish
  1. An Isolated Microculture
  2. Verbal Communication among the Amish
  3. Nonverbal Communication among the Amish
- D. The Hmong
  1. Role Relationship and Marriage
  2. Communication Patterns among the Hmong

IV. Chapter Summary

Review of Key Concepts

African-Americans: Microcultural group in the United States whose ancestors were brought to the United States as slaves.

Amish: A microcultural religiously oriented group whose members practice simple and austere living.

Ebonics: From the terms *ebony* and *phonics*, a grammatically robust and rich African-American speech pattern whose roots are in West Africa.

Hispanic: Defined by the U.S. government as a person of Cuban, Mexican, Puerto Rican, South or Central American, or other Spanish culture or origin regardless of race.

Hmong: Micro-culture belonging to the Sino-Tebetan language family and are culturally similar to the Chinese. The Hmong, which means "free people" or "mountain people" fought for the United States during the Vietnam war and many have immigrated to the United States since the end of the war.

Microculture: An identifiable group of people who share a set of values, beliefs, and behaviors and who possess a common history and verbal and nonverbal symbol system that is similar to but systematically varies from the larger, often dominant cultural milieu.

Muted Groups: Microcultures who are forced to express themselves (e.g., speak, write) within the dominant mode of expression.

Spanglish: Hybrid language combining the phonological and syntactic structures of Spanish and English.

Exercises:

1. From your computer, using your favorite browser, log-on to the internet and go to *www.census.gov*. From this home page, click on the link to *American Factfinder*. From this link you can access census data about your state, county, and/or town. From here, create a racial and ethnic profile of your hometown or the town where your university is located. Compare the racial and ethnic profile of your hometown with your university town.

2. For one week, keep a journal of microcultural groups in popular television programming. Keep track of the specific television program, date, time aired, microcultural group depicted, and specifically how the group was characterized.

Microcultural Group Television Log

Date Time Television Program Microcultural Group Depicted

_______ _____ _________________ _________________________

Comments:

Date Time Television Program Microcultural Group Depicted

_______ _____ _________________ _________________________

Comments:

Date Time Television Program Microcultural Group Depicted

_______ _____ _________________ _________________________

Comments:

Date	Time	Television Program	Microcultural Group Depicted
______	_____	________________	______________________

Comments:

Date	Time	Television Program	Microcultural Group Depicted
______	_____	________________	______________________

Comments:

Examination Preparation:

1. Based on the chapter, list and briefly explain the five criteria for membership in a microculture.

2. Identify and discuss two cultural values of Hispanics/Latinos.

3. Explain how and why microcultures often become muted groups.

4. Why are the Amish considered an isolated microculture?

5. In a sentence or two, define the following terms:

   Ebonics

   Spanglish

   Microculture

Chapter Four:
The Environmental Context

Chapter Overview:

The main point of Chapter Four is that all human communication occurs within some physical and perceptual space or environment. The physical environment includes the actual geographical location or place of communication. For instance, your class lectures occur in some real, physical location. Perceptual space is psychological, it is how we sense, perceive, and appreciate the physical location. Together the physical and perceptual environment constitute the environmental context. Chapter Four explores how culture affects our perceptions of the physical and perceptual space in which we interact with others. The first part of the chapter examines the terrestrial environment, and the built environment. The second half of the chapter focuses on the perceptual environment with emphasis on privacy and perceptions of time.

Chapter Outline (based on chapter headings)

I. Environments and Information Load

II. Culture and the Natural Environment
  A. World Views of the Natural Environment
  B. Culture and Natural Disasters

III. The Built Environment

IV. Cross-Cultural Comparisons of Housing
  A. Japanese Housing
  B. American-Navajo Housing
  C. Housing of the Marakwet of Kenya

V. Privacy
  A. Perceptions of Privacy in the United States
  B. Cross-Cultural Variations on Privacy

VI. Time
  A. Consequences of Monochronic and Polychronic Time Orientations

VII. Chapter Summary

Review of Key Concepts

Built Environment: Adaptations to the terrestrial environment, including architecture, housing, lighting, and landscaping.

Informal Space: Space defined by the movement of the interactants.

Monochronic Time Orientation: Cultural temporal orientation that stresses the compartmentalization and segmenting of measurable units of time.

Polychronic Time Orientation: Cultural temporal orientation that stresses the involvement of people and the completion of tasks as opposed to strict adherence to schedules. Time is not seen as measurable.

Privacy: The degree to which an individual can control the visual, auditory, and olfactic interaction with others.

Terrestrial Environment: The physical geography of the earth.

Exercises:

1. Take the word list below to your dormitory cafeteria during a meal hour or to the crowded student union. Carefully observe your surroundings for several minutes. Next, circle the terms in the list that best describe the environment.

Uncertain	Certain
Varied	Redundant
Complex	Simple
Novel	Familiar
Large-Scale	Small-Scale
Contrasting	Similar
Dense	Sparse
Intermittent	Continuous
Surprising	Usual
Heterogeneous	Homogeneous
Crowded	Uncrowded
Asymmetrical	Symmetrical
Immediate	Distant
Moving	Still
Rare	Common
Random	Patterned
Improbable	Probable

2. Take the word list below to a quiet place, like a local park or your dorm room when you are all alone. Carefully observe your surroundings for several minutes. Next, circle the terms in the list that best describe the environment.

Uncertain	Certain
Varied	Redundant
Complex	Simple
Novel	Familiar
Large-Scale	Small-Scale
Contrasting	Similar
Dense	Sparse
Intermittent	Continuous
Surprising	Usual
Heterogeneous	Homogeneous
Crowded	Uncrowded
Asymmetrical	Symmetrical
Immediate	Distant
Moving	Still
Rare	Common
Random	Patterned
Improbable	Probable

Having completed exercises #1 and #2, compare the types of words circled across the two environments. Words on the left hand list (e.g., complex, crowded, etc.) are descriptors of a high load environment. Words in the right hand list (e.g., simple, familiar) are descriptors of a low load environment.

3. Preferably on a weekend or a day when you have no classes or serious obligations, take off your watch, put all of your clocks in a place where they cannot be seen. Try to spend an entire day without looking at a clock. Write your reactions below. Were you comfortable not knowing what time it was? Anxious?

4. Most students sit in the same seats during class day after day. In a class where there is no assigned seating, sit somewhere else, somewhere far from where you usually sit. In fact, try sitting in the very front row in the center. How does it make you feel? Note the reactions of the people around you. Does the professor notice?

5. If you haven't already done so, complete the Privacy Questionnaire in Chapter Four. Consider your score and write down the reasons why you feel you scored either high or low in terms of your need for privacy.

Examination Preparation

1. Describe the differences between fixed and semifixed space/environment.

2. Compare and contrast monochronic and polychronic time orientations.

3. Compare and contrast high and low load environments.

4. In a few sentences, define the following terms:

   Built Environment

   Informal Space

   Information Rate

   Terrestrial Environment

Chapter Five:
The Perceptual Context

Chapter Overview:

Throughout most of the textbook, it has been pointed out that people from different cultures are different from one another. The thrust of Chapter Five emphasizes that, in many ways, regardless of culture, humans are very much alike, especially how their brains process information. Psychologists often use a computer analogy to describe how the human brain works. In other words, to better understand the human brain, think about how a computer works. Information is put into the brain (or computer), it is stored in memory, then retrieved. Continuing with the computer analogy, the brain of a human being is like the hardware of a computer and culture is the software. All human brains, regardless of culture, gather, store, and retrieve information. Culture tells them *how* to do it. This three stage process is a prerequisite for human communication and survival. The first half of Chapter Five examines the three stages of information processing. The second half focuses on how culture affects information processing, with a specific emphasis on categorization, stereotyping, ethnocentrism, and racism.

Chapter Outline (based on chapter headings)

I. Culture and Cognition

II. A Model of Human Information Processing
- A. Stage 1: Input
  - 1. Cross-Cultural Differences in Sensation and Perception
- B. Stage 2: Storage
- C. Stage 3: Retrieval
  - 1. Cross-Cultural Differences in Memory and Retrieval

III. Categorization and Mental Economy

IV. Stereotyping
- A. Racial and Ethnic Stereotypes
  - 1. American Stereotypes

V. Ethnocentrism
- A. Ethnocentrism and Intercultural Communication
- B. Ethnocentrism and Racism

VI. Chapter Summary

Review of Key Concepts

Categorization: Classifying or sorting of perceived information into distinct groups.

Cognition: Higher mental processes, such as perception and memory.

Episodic Memory: A component of long-term memory where private individual memories are stored.

Ethnocentrism: Tendency to place one's own group or ethnicity in a position of centrality and worth while creating negative attitudes and behaviors towards other groups.

Long-term Memory: Cognitive storage area where large amounts of information are held relatively permanently.

Memory: The storage of information in the human brain over time.

Perception: The mental interpretation of external stimuli via sensation.

Recall/Retrieval: To call to the mind, or recollection of, stored information.

Semantic Memory: A part of long-term memory where general information such as how to read and write and the meanings of words are stored.

Sensation: Gathering of visual, auditory, olfactic, haptic, and taste stimuli/information.

Short-term Memory: Cognitive storage area where small amounts of information are held for short periods of time, usually less than 20 seconds.

Stereotypes: A subset of categorizing and involving the attribution of characteristics of a group to an individual based on individual's membership in that group. Stereotypes are categories with an attitude.

Exercises:

1. Without thinking about it for more than a few seconds, write down the first three things that come to mind when you hear:

Jew: ____________ ____________ ____________

African-American: ____________ ____________ ____________

Native-American: ____________ ____________ ____________

White (Caucasian): ____________ ____________ ____________
Gay/Lesbian: ____________ ____________ ____________

Catholic: ____________ ____________ ____________

Hispanic: ____________ ____________ ____________

Now, being ***as honest as you can*** with yourself, on a scale of 1 to 10, rate each of the words you wrote down for each group; 1 meaning that the word is very positive, 10 meaning that the word is very negative. Consider how you describe each group.

2. Closely examine these two optical illusions.

Do you see a face or the word liar?

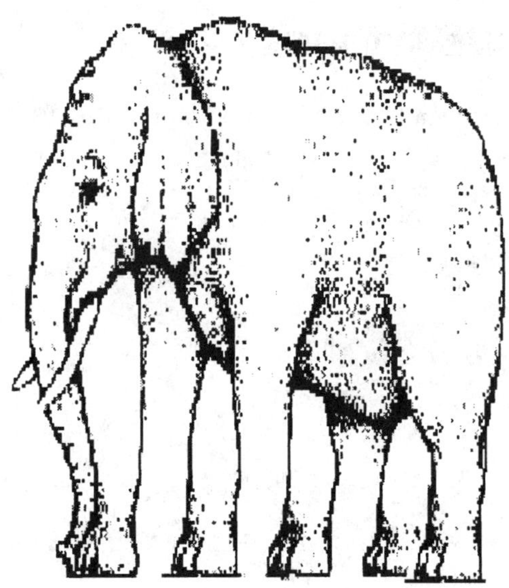

How many legs does the elephant have?

3. What kind of memory are you using when you recall the following? Circle the correct type of memory.

a.	Pizza place phone number	short-term	episodic long-term	semantic long-term
b.	First grade teacher's name	short-term	episodic long-term	semantic long-term
c.	The spelling of your state	short-term	episodic long-term	semantic long-term
d.	Your Dad's middle name	short-term	episodic long-term	semantic long-term
e.	The meaning of the word "ear"	short-term	episodic long-term	semantic long-term

Answers

a. short-term (unless you had it memorized from frequent usage, then it would be episodic long-term).
b. episodic long-term.
c. semantic long-term.
d. episodic long-term.
e. semantic long-term.

Examination Preparation:

1. List and discuss the three stages of information processing.

2. What's the difference between ethnocentrism and racism. How are they related?

3. List and define four types of mental categories.

4. In a sentence or two, define the following terms:

   Outgroup Homogeneity Effect:

   Illusory Correlation Principle

   Perception

   Sensory Register

Chapter Six:
The Sociorelational Context

Chapter Overview:

The sociorelational context refers to the group memberships to which we belong. All people of all cultures belong to groups; some are involuntary, such as sex and age, and some are voluntary, such as occupation or religion. When we interact with others, particularly those people we do not know very well, we often tailor our verbal and nonverbal messages to the group memberships of the other person. Our social relationships with others are significantly influenced by the groups to which we belong, hence the term *sociorelational* context.

The first part of Chapter Six looks at the various types of groups, such as membership and nonmembership, ingroups and outgroups, voluntary and involuntary, and reference groups. The second part of the chapter focuses on role relationships, role differentiation and social stratification. When we join a group, we take on a role. Roles are prescriptions for behavior; they prescribe with whom, about what, and how we interact with others. The last half of the chapter examines family groups and sex groups across cultures.

Chapter Outline (based on chapter headings)

I. Dimensions of Group Variability
   A. Membership and Nonmembership Groups
   B. Ingroups and Outgroups
   C. Reference Groups

II. Role Relationships, Role Differentiation, and Social Stratification
   A. Role Relationships
   B. Role Differentiation and Social Stratification

III. Family Groups

IV. Sex and Gender Groups
   A. Gender Stereotypes

V. Sex and Gender Roles Across Cultures
   A. Morocco
   B. Japan
   C. India

VI. Chapter Summary

Review of Key Concepts

Gender: A socially constructed and learned creation usually associated with one's sex; masculinity and femininity. People are born into a sex group, but learn to become masculine or feminine. The meaning of gender stems from the particular culture's value system.

Ingroup: A membership group whose norms, goals, and values shape the behavior of the members. Extreme ingroups see the actions of an outgroup as threatening to the ingroup.

Involuntary Membership Group: A group to which a person belongs and has no choice but to belong, such as a person's sex, race, and age group.

Involuntary Nonmembership Group: A group to which a person does not belong because of ineligibility.

Membership Group: A group to which a person belongs where there is regular interaction among members who perceive of themselves as members.

Outgroup: A group whose attributes are dissimilar from an ingroup and who opposes the realization of ingroup goals.

Reference Group: A group to which a person may or may not belong, but identifies in some way with the values and goals of the group.

Role: One's relative hierarchical position or rank in a group. A role is a prescribed set of behaviors that are expected in order to fulfill the role.

Sex Role: A prescribed set of behaviors assigned to different sexes.

Social Identity: The total combination of one's group roles. A part of the individual's self-concept that is derived from the person's membership in groups.

Social Stratification: A culture's organization of roles into a hierarchical vertical status structure.

Exercises:

1. For each of the following roles you assume, list at least eight behaviors that are expected of you:

	Student	Brother/Sister	Son/Daughter
1.	________________	____________________	________________
2.	________________	____________________	________________
3.	________________	____________________	________________
4.	________________	____________________	________________
5.	________________	____________________	________________
6.	________________	____________________	________________
7.	________________	____________________	________________
8.	________________	____________________	________________

2. Paired with another member of your class, compare your role expectations listed above. How are the behavioral expectations similar or different? Which of the expectations are cultural and which are unique to you?

3. Role Switching: With someone you know very well (e.g., brother/sister, best friend, roommate, etc) switch roles; that is, act as if you are the other person by imitating their patterns of verbal and nonverbal behavior. Of course, the other person will imitate you. Allow this role-switching exercise to continue for a while. This exercise will give each of you an idea of how you are perceived in your role.

Examination Preparation:

1. Choose two cultures, identify them, and compare and contrast sex roles in each.

2. Define and discuss the idea of role differentiation.

3. Carefully articulate the difference between sex and gender.

4. In a sentence or two, define the following terms:

    Role

    Reference Group

    Sex Role/Gender

    Social Stratification

Chapter Seven: The Verbal Code

Chapter Overview:

Human language may be the most distinguishing feature that separates humans from the rest of the living beings on the planet. Other living beings are larger, stronger, faster, and smaller, but no other living being has the capacity for language. Because of language, humans are probably the most powerful beings on the planet. There are two main ideas about language presented in Chapter Seven. The first is that human language is biological. Just as humans have hands and feet, we have human language. Many contemporary linguists (people who study language) believe that humans are born with the capacity for language. They believe that language acquisition is encoded in our DNA, as is our ability to walk upright or have hair. The second main point of this chapter is that while all of the languages of the world seem very different from each other, they are actually very much alike. All languages are comprised of a set of sounds (like the alphabet), combined with a set of rules (grammar) that take on meaning. All languages share several common components. In addition to these two main points, the chapter also examines different language styles. How people use language differs considerably from culture to culture. In the United States, we have a tendency to be very direct and personal in our use of language. We also tend to find silence uncomfortable. The Japanese, on the other hand, tend to be very indirect, formal, and are generally comfortable with silence. The chapter closes with a discussion of how people create and manage their ethnic identity through language. In this case, African-Americans' use of Ebonics is highlighted.

Chapter Outline (Based on chapter headings)

I. The Relationship Between Language and Culture
- A. The Sapir-Whorf Hypothesis

II. The Structure of Human Language
- A. Sounds and Symbols
- B. Syntax and Universal Grammar
- C. Universals of Language
- D. Generative Grammar

III. Elaborated and Restricted Codes

IV. Cross-Cultural Communication Styles
- A. Direct and Indirect Styles
- B. Elaborate, Exacting, and Succinct Styles
- C. Personal and Contextual Styles
- D. Instrumental and Affective Styles

V. Language and Ethnic Identity

VI. Chapter Summary

Review of Key Concepts

Affective Style: Communication manner where the process of interaction is emphasized placing the burden of understanding on both the speaker and the listener. Relies heavily on nonverbal cues.

Contextual Style: Role-centered mode of speaking where one's choice of messages is influenced by one's relative status in the conversation.

Direct Style: Manner of speaking where one employs overt expressions of intention.

Elaborated Code: A cultural context wherein the speakers of a language have a variety of linguistic options open to them in order to explicitly communicate their intent via verbal messages.

Elaborate Style: Mode of speaking which emphasizes rich expressive language.

Exacting Style: Manner of speaking where persons say no more or less than is needed to communicate a point.

Generative Grammar: The idea that from a finite set of rules, a speaker of any language can create or generate a countably infinite number of sentences, many of which have never before been uttered.

Indirect Style: Manner of speaker wherein the intentions of the speakers are hidden or only hinted at during interaction.

Instrumental Style: Sender-focused manner of speaker that is goal and outcome oriented. Instrumental speakers "use" communication to achieve some goal or purpose.

Language: A systematic set of sounds, combined with a set of rules, for the sole purpose of communicating.

Personal Style: Manner of speaking relying on the use of personal pronouns that stresses informality and symmetrical power relationships.

Restricted Code: A cultural context wherein the speakers of a language are limited as to what they can say or do verbally. A restricted code is a status oriented system.

Succinct Style: Manner of very concise speaking often accompanied with silence.

Symbol: Arbitrarily selected and learned stimulus representing something else.

Universal Grammar: The idea that all languages share a common rule structure or grammar that is innate in human beings, regardless of culture.

Exercises:

1. With a group of three or four other students in your class, write a short play where the characters are from different cultures. As you write the lines, assign a different language style to each character (e.g., direct, indirect, personal, contextual, etc.).

2. In the space provided below, list three of the most used slang words that you and your friends use (or used) and write their definitions (e.g., "Chillin" means to relax or hang-out). Compare your words and definitions with other persons in the class.

Word	Definition
________________	________________________________
________________	________________________________
________________	________________________________

Examination Preparation:

1. What is meant by the assertion that "language is biological?"

2. What is the central thesis of the Sapir Whorf Hypothesis?

3. How do ethnic groups use language to create their ethnic identity?

4. In a sentence or two, define the following terms:

   Universal Grammar:

   Generative Grammar:

   Direct Style:

   Elaborate Style:

Chapter Eight
The Nonverbal Code

Chapter Overview:

When humans communicate with each other, they use both a verbal and a nonverbal code. Many communication scholars believe that the majority of the messages we send are nonverbal rather than verbal. The way you stand, the tone of your voice, the space between you and the other person, how you smell, where you touch the other person all send messages. Recall (from Chapter One) that a fundamental assumption about intercultural communication is that it is primarily a nonverbal act between people. Just as verbal languages vary the world over, nonverbal messages vary across cultures. The same gesture in one culture may carry very different meaning in another culture.

The majority of Chapter Eight focuses on several distinct channels of nonverbal communication. The chapter opens with a definition of nonverbal communication then moves onto a comparison of the verbal and nonverbal code. Next, the chapter profiles kinesics, paralanguage, proxemics, haptics, olfactics, physical appearance and dress, and chronemics. Finally, the chapter ends with a very interesting and applicable theory about nonverbal communication called Nonverbal Expectancy Violations Theory.

Chapter Review (based on chapter headings)

I. Definitions of Nonverbal Communication

II. The Relationship Between Verbal and Nonverbal Codes.
   A. Formal versus Informal Code Systems

III. Channels of Nonverbal Communication
   A. Kinesics
      1. Emblems and Illustrators
      2. Affect Displays: Facial Expressions of Emotion
      3. Cross-Racial Recognition of Faces
      4. Regulators
      5. Adaptors
   B. Paralanguage
   C. Proxemics
   D. Haptics
   E. Olfactics
   F. Physical Appearance and Dress
   G. Chronemics

IV. Nonverbal Expectancy Violations Theory
    A. Cultural Contexts and Nonverbal Expectancies

V. Chapter Summary

Review of Key Concepts

Adaptors: Mostly unconscious nonverbal actions that satisfy physiological or psychological needs, such as scratching an itch.

Affect Displays: Nonverbal presentations of emotion, primarily communicated through facial expressions.

Chronemics: The perception and use of time.

Emblems: Primarily hand gestures that have a direct verbal translation. Can be used to repeat or to substitute for verbal communication.

Haptics: Nonverbal communication through physical contact or touch.

Kinesics: General category of body motion, including emblems, illustrators, affect displays, and adaptors.

Nonverbal Expectancy Violations Theory: Theory that posits that people hold expectations about the nonverbal behavior of others. When these expectations are violated, people evaluate the violation positively or negatively, depending on the source of the violation.

Olfactics: The perception and use of smell, scent, and odor.

Paralanguage: Characteristics of the voice, such as pitch, rhythm, intensity, volume, and rate.

Proxemics: The perception and use of space, including territoriality and personal space.

Exercises:

1. Chapter Eight mentions the idea that Americans seem obsessed with the smell of the human body. In the space provided below, list all of the products you use that alter the smell of your body (e.g., toothpaste, shampoo, fabric softener). Next to the product name, describe its odor.

Body Product	Odor Description
____________________	____
____________________	____
____________________	____
____________________	____
____________________	____
____________________	____
____________________	____
____________________	____
____________________	____
____________________	____
____________________	____
____________________	____
____________________	____
____________________	____
____________________	____
____________________	____
____________________	____
____________________	____

2. Using the scheme below indicate (by circling Yes or No) if you have been touched by the person indicated in the last two weeks.

Body Location	Best Friend		Roommate		Boy/Girl Friend	
1. Head	Yes	No	Yes	No	Yes	No
2. Face	Yes	No	Yes	No	Yes	No
3. Neck	Yes	No	Yes	No	Yes	No
4. Shoulders (either)	Yes	No	Yes	No	Yes	No
5. Arm (either)	Yes	No	Yes	No	Yes	No
6. Hand	Yes	No	Yes	No	Yes	No
7. Chest	Yes	No	Yes	No	Yes	No
8. Back	Yes	No	Yes	No	Yes	No
9. Stomach	Yes	No	Yes	No	Yes	No
10. Groin Area	Yes	No	Yes	No	Yes	No
11. Leg/Thigh	Yes	No	Yes	No	Yes	No
12. Leg/Calf	Yes	No	Yes	No	Yes	No
13. Buttocks	Yes	No	Yes	No	Yes	No

Compare touch ratios by relationship. Who touches you the most? The least?

3. If you haven't already done so, complete the Personal Report of Olfactic Perception and Sensitivity (PROPS) scale. Considering your score, are you more or less sensitive to the smell of others? Why?

Examination Preparation

1. Discuss any three of the fundamental assumptions of Nonverbal Expectancy Violations Theory.

2. What is the difference between an emblem and an illustrator?

3. What is meant by "own race recognition bias"?

4. In a sentence or two, define the following terms:

   Kinesics

   Haptics

   Paralanguage

   Regulators

Chapter Nine:
Developing Intercultural Relationships

Chapter Overview:

Many social scientists believe that the only way we can know ourselves is through others. In other words, other people, especially those with whom we are intimate, define who we are. Think, for a moment, about three words that describe you. Next, how do you know? How do you know that these terms are accurate descriptors of you? The way you know is by the feedback of others. For example, if you consider yourself a good student, how do you know? You know, because teachers and professors have told you so by providing positive feedback, in the form of good grades, on exams and papers.

In all cultures people establish, maintain, and terminate relationships with others. Chapter Nine focuses on five variables that are especially important in establishing and maintaining intercultural relationships, including uncertainty reduction, intercultural communication apprehension, sociocommunicative style, empathy, and similarity. In addition, the chapter examines perceptions of relational intimacy across cultures and marital relationships among differing cultures.

Chapter Outline (based on chapter headings)

I. Communication and Uncertainty
   A. Uncertainty Reduction and Intercultural Communication Apprehension
   B. Assessing Sociocommunicative Style

II. Empathy and Similarity in Relationship Development

III. Empathy

IV. Similarity

V. Perceptions of Relational Intimacy Across Cultures
   A. Eastern and Western Cultures and Relationships

VI. Marital Relationships
   A. Intercultural and Interracial Marriages
   B. Mate Selection Across Cultures
   C. Arranged Marriages
   D. Marital Dissolution and Divorce Across Cultures

VII. Chapter Summary

Review of Key Concepts

Assertiveness: An individual's ability to make requests, actively disagree, and express positive or negative personal rights and feelings.

Relational Empathy: Shared meaning and harmonization that is the result of the interaction of two people.

Responsiveness: An individual's ability to be sensitive to the communication of others, including providing feedback, comforting communication, and listening.

Sociocommunicative Style: Degree of assertiveness and responsiveness during communication.

Third Culture: That which is created when a dyad consisting of persons from different cultures come together and establish relational empathy.

Uncertainty: The amount of predictability in a communication situation.

Uncertainty Reduction Theory: Theory whose major premise is that when strangers first meet, their primary goal is to reduce uncertainty.

Exercises:

1. This is an exercise in similarity. Initially answer the questions below. Now, interview a close friend of yours, asking him/her the same questions. Compare your answers to your friend's.

1. Your age ______ Your friend's age _______

2. Your major _______ Your friend's major ________

3. Your native language _______________ Your friend's native language ___________

4. Favorite style of music ______________ Your friend's favorite style of music ________

5. Your height ____________ Your friend's height __________

6. Your year in school __________ Your friend's year in school __________

7. Do you drink alcohol? _________ Does your friend drink alcohol? __________

8. Do you smoke? _________ Does your friend smoke? ____________

9. Are you athletic? __________ Is your friend athletic? ____________

10. Are you religious? __________ Is your friend religious? ____________

2. Imagine that you are about to send to your local newspaper a "personal ad." A personal ad is where you describe the type of person you are and the type of person you're looking for in a potential mate. Below, write your ad. Next, compare the way you describe yourself with the kinds of attributes you're looking for in someone else. Chances are very good that they are very similar.

3. If you have not already done so, complete the Sociocommunicative Style survey in Chapter Nine. Consider your assertiveness score. What makes you assertive (or not)? Consider your responsiveness score. What makes you responsive (or not)?

Examination Preparation:

1. Discuss three of the fundamental assumptions of Uncertainty Reduction Theory.

2. Define and discuss the idea of relational empathy and third culture building.

3. List and discuss two of the major differences between Eastern and Western relationships.

4. In a sentence or two, define the following terms:

   Assertiveness

   Responsiveness

   Intercultural Communication Apprehension

Chapter Ten: Intercultural Communication in Organizations

Chapter Overview:

The basic tenet of Chapter Ten is that there is no universal theory of management. The management theories and practices that are taught and applied in one country, in most cases, do not apply in another country. Managers from the United States are often culpable of exercising American "tried and true" management strategies when they manage people abroad. In many cases, such strategies fail.

Much of what has been discussed so far in the text can be applied within organizational settings. One of the arguments made in Chapter Ten is that an understanding of a particular culture's cultural, micro-cultural, environmental, perceptual, and sociorelational contexts can be very informative when trying to understand how organizations function within a culture. In other words, the dimensions of cultural variability (i.e., individualism/collectivism, high-low context, etc.) that are practiced in the larger cultural context, are probably applied similarly within organizations. For example, in a high power-distance culture like Mexico, the status difference between managers and employees is distinct and well-defined. In individualistic cultures, like the United States, employees are often rewarded for their individual initiative and resourcefulness and often participate in decision-making.

In addition to highlighting the cultural, micro-cultural, environmental, perceptual, and sociorelational contexts, Chapter Ten takes a close look at management practices in Japan, Germany, and Mexico, three of our biggest trading partners. Finally, the chapter closes with a discussion of conflict in organizations with special attention on those factors that facilitate conflict.

Chapter Overview (based on chapter headings)

I. Intercultural Management
   - A. Cultural Context
   - B. Environmental Context
   - C. Perceptual Context
   - D. Sociorelational Context
   - E. Verbal and Nonverbal Codes
   - F. Intercultural Relations

II. Management Practices Across Cultures
   - A. Japanese Management Practices
   - B. German Management Practices
   - C. Management Practices in Mexico

III. Conflict in Organizations

IV. Chapter Summary

Review of Key Concepts

Cultural context: An accumulated pattern of values, beliefs, and behavior held by an identifiable group of people with a common verbal and nonverbal symbol system.

Environmental Context: The geographical and psychological location of communication within some cultural context.

Individual Factors: Individual factors that facilitate conflict, including cognitive simplicity/rigidity, ingroup bias, insecurity/frustration, and divergent behaviors.

Intermediary Factors: Contextual or situational factors that facilitate conflict, including segregation/contact, intergroup salience, and status differentials.

Organizational Culture: An organized pattern of values, beliefs, behaviors, and communication channels held by the members of an organization.

Perceptual Context: The cognitive process by which persons gather, store, and retrieve information.

Power Distance: The extent to which less powerful members of a particular culture accept and expect that power within the culture will be distributed unequally.

Societal Factors: Factors that facilitate conflict, including a history of subjugation, structural inequities, and minority group strength.

Sociorelational Context: The roles that one assumes within a culture; roles are defined by verbal and nonverbal messages.

Exercises:

1. Go to your college/university library and find a current book on management (perhaps a textbook that is used in management classes at your college/university). Look throughout the book and find examples of (a) individualistic, (b) low power distance, (c) weak uncertainty avoidance, and (d) dominant cultural values, as they pertain to management.

2. Interview an administrator at your college/university or manager at a local organization. Ask him/her the following questions:

    a) Do you encourage your employees to participate in decision-making?

    b) Do you encourage and reward self-initiative in your employees?

    c) Which of the following best describes your management philosophy:

- a manager is like a teacher he/she offers help and guidance when needed, but generally lets the employees do their job on their own.

- a manager prescribes to employees what is to be done, and how it is to be done, and then watches over the employees to make sure they are performing accordingly.

Question “a” and “c” tap into power-distance. Most American managers probably answer yes to “a” and see themselves as a teacher more than a taskmaster.

Question “b” taps into individualism. Most American managers probably encourage self-initiative.

3. Do some thorough research on a conflict that has regional, state, national, or international significance. Then, write a brief description, with examples, of how the following factors contribute to the conflict.

Cognitive simplicity/rigidity

Ingroup bias

Insecurity/frustration

Divergent behavior

Segregation and contact

Intergroup salience

Status discrepancy

History of subjugation

Structural inequities

Minority group strength

Examination Preparation:

1. List three managerial practices of German managers.

2. List three managerial practices of Japanese managers.

3. List three managerial practices of Mexican managers.

Chapter Eleven: Acculturation and Culture Shock

Chapter Overview:

Whenever people travel or move to a different culture, they will typically experience a period of adjustment. By entering a different culture people are faced with different values, behavioral patterns, and communication styles. For most people, it takes time to adjust to their new surroundings. In Chapter Eleven, two concepts associated with entering into a different culture are discussed, including acculturation and culture shock. *Acculturation* is the term used to describe what happens when people from one culture enter into a different culture. Technically, acculturation is the process whereby you adapt to a new culture by adopting its values, attitudes, and practices. Not everyone acculturates the same way. *Culture shock* is a multifaceted experience resulting from the stress associated with entering a new culture. Most people experience some degree of culture shock as they become acculturated to their new environment. Often times people feel alienated, stressed out, and depressed. Usually, these feelings of culture shock are temporary.

Chapter Outline (based on chapter headings)

I. Acculturation
   - A. Acculturative Stress
   - B. A Model of Acculturation
   - C. Modes of Acculturation
   - D. Acculturation in the United States

II. Culture Shock
   - A. Models of Culture Shock
   - B. "W Curve" Models of Culture Shock
   - C. Strategies for Managing Culture Shock
   - D. Assessing Culture Shock

III. Chapter Summary

Review of Key Concepts

Acculturation: The process of cultural change that results from ongoing contact between two or more culturally different groups.

Acculturative Stress: The anxiety and tension associated with acculturation.

Assimilation: The degree to which an individual takes on the behaviors and language habits and practices the basic rules and norms of the host culture while relinquishing ties with the native culture.

Cultural Transmutation: Mode of acculturation in which the individual chooses to identify with a third cultural group (microculture) that materializes out of the native and host cultural groups.

Culture Shock: The effects associated with the tension and anxiety of entering into a new culture, combined with the sensations of loss, confusion, and powerlessness resulting from the forfeiture of cultural norms and social rituals.

Integration: Mode of acculturation in which the individual develops a kind of bicultural orientation that successfully blends and synthesizes cultural dimensions from both groups while maintaining an identity in each group.

Re-Entry Shock: The effects associated with the tension and anxiety of returning to one's native culture after an extended stay in a foreign culture.

Exercises

1. In many ways, leaving home and going to college is like entering a new culture. You are in a different environment, eating different food, sleeping in a different bed, interacting with different people, and taking classes. Think back to your first days and weeks as a college freshman. In the space provided below, write out some of the experiences you had during the different phases of culture shock.

   Tourist Phase:

   Culture Shock Phase:

Adjustment Phase:

Adaptation/Acculturation Phase:

2. Figure 11-3 in Chapter Eleven points out the various factors that affect the degree of culture shock you might experience. Using Figure 11-3, and in the space provided below, list the factors that personally affect you.

Intrapersonal Factors:

Organismic/Biological Factors:

Interpersonal Factors:

Geopolitical Factors:

Spatial/Temporal Factors:

Cultural Similarity:

Host Culture Attitudes/Policies:

Quality of Information:

Control Factors:

3. If you are Hispanic or African-American, and have not already done so, complete the Hispanic Acculturation or the African-American Acculturation scale. Below write your score and list some of the reasons for your score.

Acculturation Score: __________

Examination Preparation:

1. Compare and contrast the terms 'acculturation' and 'acculturative stress.'

2. List and define the modes of acculturation.

3. In a sentence or two, define the following terms:

   Culture Shock

   Assimilation

   Re-Entry Shock

Chapter Twelve: Intercultural Competence

Chapter Overview:

One of the main goals of this book is to help you become a competent intercultural communicator. Chapter Twelve is devoted to a concept we call *intercultural communication competence,* which is defined as the degree to which you effectively adapt your verbal and nonverbal messages to the appropriate cultural context. When you communicate with someone from a different culture, you will have to adjust and modify the kinds of verbal and nonverbal messages you send. Being a competent intercultural communicator requires you to *know* something about the person with whom you are communicating, that you are *motivated* to communicate with him/her, and that you have verbal and nonverbal *skills* in order to encode and decode messages appropriately. Chapter Twelve is organized around four components of intercultural competence, including a knowledge component, an affective component, a psychomotor component, and situational features component. Chapter Twelve also gives you the opportunity to assess the knowledge and affective components of your intercultural competence.

Chapter Outline: (based on chapter headings)

I. Intercultural Competence
   - A. A Model of Intercultural Competence
   - B. The Knowledge Component
   - C. The Affective Component
   - D. The Psychomotor Component
   - E. Situational Features
   - F. Intercultural Training Programs

II. Chapter Summary

Review of Key Concepts

Affective Component: Approach-avoidance tendencies during intercultural communication. The extent to which one experiences intercultural communication apprehension and one's willingness to communicate.

Intercultural Competence: The ability to adapt one's verbal and nonverbal messages to the appropriate cultural context.

Intercultural Willingness to Communicate: Predisposition to initiate intercultural interaction with persons from different cultures even when completely free to choose whether or not to communicate.

Knowledge Component: The extent of one's awareness of another's culture's values etc. Also the extent to which one is cognitively simple, rigid, and ethnocentric.

Psychomotor Features: The extent to which one can translate cultural knowledge into appropriate verbal and nonverbal performance and role enactment.

Situational Features: The extent to which the environmental context, previous contact, status differential and third-party intervention affect one's competence during intercultural communication.

Exercises

1. If you haven't already done so, complete the Cross-Cultural Awareness scale in Chapter Twelve. If you scored below 35, list three things you might do to increase your cultural awareness:

    1.

    2.

    3.

2. If you haven't already done so, complete the Intercultural Willingness to Communicate scale in Chapter Twelve. If you scored below 350, consider and then list the reasons why you think you are not willing to communicate with others from different cultures. What might you do to increase your willingness?

Score:__________

Examination Preparation:

1. Identify and discuss the elements of the knowledge component of the intercultural competence model.

2. Identify and discuss the elements of the affective component of the intercultural competence model.

3. Identify and discuss the elements of the psychomotor component of the intercultural competence model.